THE DIVERSITY
OF SPECIES

MICHAEL BRIGHT

www.heinemannlibrary.co.uk
Visit our website to find out more information about **Heinemann Library** books.

To order:
☎ Phone 44 (0) 1865 888066
▤ Send a fax to 44 (0) 1865 314091
Visit the Heinemann Bookshop at www.heinemannlibrary.co.uk to browse our catalogue and order online.

Heinemann Library is an imprint of Capstone Global Library Limited, a company incorporated in England and Wales having its registered office at 7 Pilgrim Street, London, EC4V 6LB – Registered company number: 6695582

"Heinemann" is a registered trademark of Pearson Education Limited, under licence to Capstone Global Library Limited.

Text © Capstone Global Library Limited 2009
First published in hardback in 2009
Paperback edition first published in 2010
The moral rights of the proprietor have been asserted.

Edited by Pollyanna Poulter
Designed by Steven Mead and Q2A Creative Solutions
Illustrated by International Mapping and Stuart Jackson-Carter/The Art Agency
Picture research by Elizabeth Alexander
Originated by Dot Gradations
Printed in China by Leo Paper Group

ISBN 978-0-431064-71-0 (hardback)
13 12 11 10 09
10 9 8 7 6 5 4 3 2 1

ISBN 978-0-431064-77-2 (paperback)
14 13 12 11 10
10 9 8 7 6 5 4 3 2 1

British Library Cataloguing-in-Publication Data
Bright, Michael
The diversity of species. - (Timeline : life on Earth)
1. Biodiversity - Juvenile literature
I. Title
578.7

A full catalogue record for this book is available from the British Library.

Acknowledgments
We would like to thank the following for permission to reproduce photographs: © Aaron Rundus p. **45**; © Alamy: p. **6** (David Forster), p. **10** (Mary Evans Picture Library), p. **11** (Brandon Cole Marine Photography), p. **26** (Steve Bloom Images), p. **27** (Kitt Cooper-Smith), p. **41** (blickwinkel), p. **44** (Gallo Images); © ardea.com: p. **37** (John Cancalosi); © Corbis: p. **30** (John Conrad), p. **39** and p. **40** (Joe McDonald), p. **42**; © Dreamstime.com: p. **15 right** (3dclipartsde); © FLPA: p. **5** (Minden Pictures/FLPA), p. **35** (Roger Tidman); © Getty Images: p. **33** (Norbert Wu), p. **47** (National Geographic); © Imagequestmarine.com: p. **33** (Michael Aw), p. **34** (Masa Ushioda), p. **46** (Peter Batson); © Istockphoto: pp. **4, 14, 22, 32,** and **38 chapter openers** and all **panel backgrounds** (Elzbieta Sekowska), p. **15 middle right**, p. **15 middle left** (Chanyut Sribua-rawd), p. **15 far right** (christian darkin); © 2008 Jupiterimages Corporation: p. **15 left** and **far left**; © Naturepl.com: p. **24** (RICHARD KIRBY), p. **29** (Angelo Gandolfi); © Photolibrary: p. **12-13** (David Fox), p. **19** (Dupc/David Haring), p. **36** (Satoshi Kuribayashi), p. **43** (Richard Kirby); © Science Photo Library: p. **20** (Sheila Terry), p. **21** (ANDREW SYRED), p. **23** (JOHN DURHAM), p. **31** (A. BARRINGTON BROWN); © The Bridgeman Art Library: p. **16** (Bibliotheque de la Faculte de Medecine, Paris, France, Archives Charmet); © Tips Images: p. **8** (Sunset), p. **30** (Bildagentur).

Cover photograph of peacock reproduced with permission of © NHPA (Guy Edwardes).

We would like to thank Mandy Holloway and Gavin Fidler for their invaluable help in the preparation of this book.

Every effort has been made to contact copyright holders of material reproduced in this book. Any omissions will be rectified in subsequent printings if notice is given to the publishers.

Disclaimer
All the Internet addresses (URLs) given in this book were valid at the time of going to press. However, due to the dynamic nature of the Internet, some addresses may have changed, or sites may have changed or ceased to exist since publication. While the author and Publishers regret any inconvenience this may cause readers, no responsibility for any such changes can be accepted by either the author or the Publishers.

CONTENTS

Some words are printed in bold, **like this**. You can find out what they mean in the glossary.

DIVERSITY OF LIFE

Life on Earth

The number of different types of living things on Earth is staggering. There are an estimated 14 million **species** of plants, animals, algae, fungi, and **bacteria**. Approximately 1.75 million of these have been described by science. Scientists believe that most species have yet to be discovered, because new ones are turning up every day. In a patch of Amazon rainforest no larger than a football pitch, biologists estimate that there are 60,000 species of insects and spiders alone. Eighty percent of these will be new to science. In 2004, a single expedition, led by The Nature Conservancy to East Kalimantan, Indonesia, discovered new species of fish, miniature freshwater crabs, snails, and begonias. The scientists also discovered a pure white 6.5 cm- (2.5 in-) long cave millipede, and a monster 10 cm- (4 in-) long cave cockroach. They were found in and around Borneo's cave systems. Almost every plant and animal found was new to science.

You may think fish, insects, and other small creatures would be easier to overlook than a large **mammal**. But in recent years there have been some remarkable finds. In the forests of

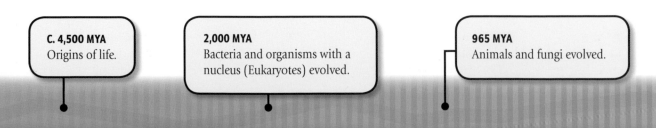

C. 4,500 MYA
Origins of life.

2,000 MYA
Bacteria and organisms with a nucleus (Eukaryotes) evolved.

965 MYA
Animals and fungi evolved.

| 5,000 MYA | | 2,500 MYA | | 1,000 MYA |

MYA = million years ago

Cambodia, Vietnam, and Laos several species of deer, including a giant muntjac, were reported in the 1990s. Throughout the world, 38 new species of monkey have been discovered since 1980.

This includes a new titi monkey from South America. It is known as the GoldenPalace.com monkey after its name was auctioned on the worldwide web for research funding!

The rate at which new species are being discovered has led some scientists to suggest that the world total could be higher still, upwards of 100 million species. This amazing diversity of living things, of course, did not appear overnight. The huge diversity of life we see today is the result of 4 billion years of evolution.

ESTIMATED AMOUNT OF SPECIES ON EARTH

Protoctists (algae, protozoa, etc.) 80,000

Plants 270,000

Bacteria and Fungi 78,000

Animals:
invertebrates 1,272,000
vertebrates 52,000

Unknown Species 12,250,000

▲ *This pie chart shows that scientists believe the overwhelming number of living things on our planet have yet to be discovered.*

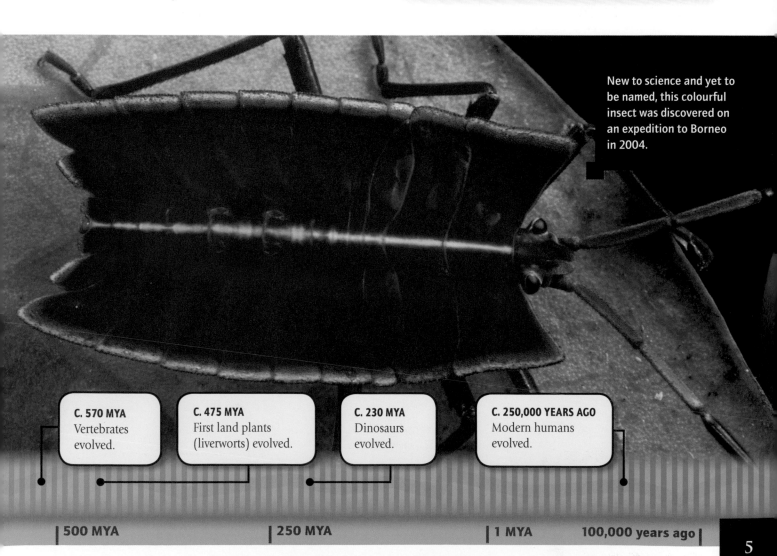

New to science and yet to be named, this colourful insect was discovered on an expedition to Borneo in 2004.

C. 570 MYA
Vertebrates evolved.

C. 475 MYA
First land plants (liverworts) evolved.

C. 230 MYA
Dinosaurs evolved.

C. 250,000 YEARS AGO
Modern humans evolved.

| 500 MYA | 250 MYA | 1 MYA | 100,000 years ago |

What is life?

Life is an extraordinary thing. Basically, it's a whole lot of chemistry – living things made from carbon-based chemicals. The first signs of life appeared on Earth about 4,000 million years ago. It was simple at first, with no more than a few of those chemicals working together. But then those bundles of chemicals began to reproduce or replicate (copy themselves). As they reproduced, mistakes and modifications of the chemicals began to creep in. Some bundles survived the changes, others did not. As a consequence, life became increasingly more complicated. Bundles of chemicals got together with others and formed **cells**. Cells got together to form **organisms**. Eventually, the organisms ranged from the simple to the complex – from something as lowly as a bacterium to a living thing as complex as a human being. Over millions of years, living things not only survived but also thrived in every **habitat** that appeared on the planet.

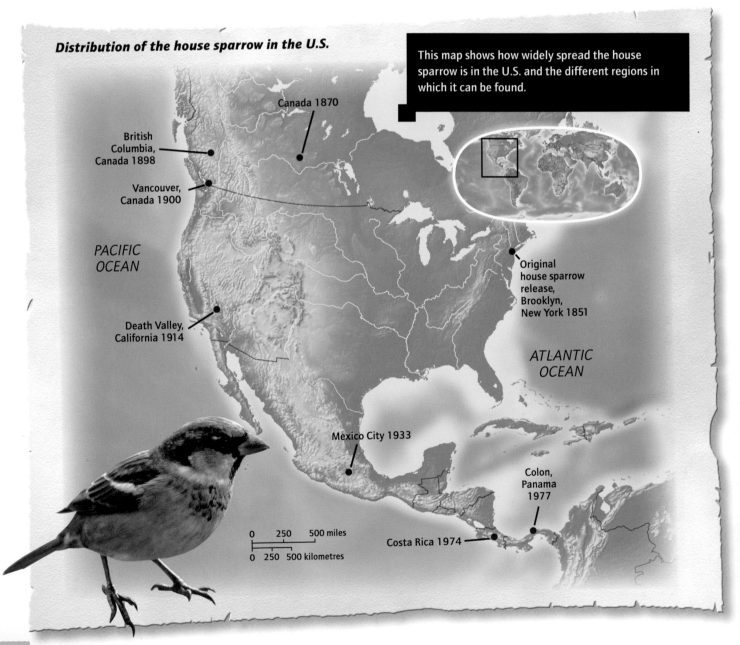

Distribution of the house sparrow in the U.S.

This map shows how widely spread the house sparrow is in the U.S. and the different regions in which it can be found.

Canada 1870

British Columbia, Canada 1898

Vancouver, Canada 1900

PACIFIC OCEAN

Death Valley, California 1914

Original house sparrow release, Brooklyn, New York 1851

ATLANTIC OCEAN

Mexico City 1933

Colon, Panama 1977

Costa Rica 1974

0   250   500 miles

0   250   500 kilometres

Evolution

Evolution is the natural process by which organisms change over time. The changes are not the same as rocks being worn down by erosion, or deciduous trees losing their leaves. Evolutionary changes occur during the process of reproduction (also called replication) of all living things. It means that an individual organism cannot evolve, because the changes go beyond its lifespan. These changes occur in **populations** of animals – species, families, **orders** – and are **inherited** via the **genes** from one **generation** to the next. As we shall see, changes can be caused by all manner of natural or artificial events – **predation**, **competition**, environmental change, pollution, and even **mutations** in the genes themselves. For the past century and a half, scientists have been studying these changes and gathering evidence that supports the theory of biological evolution. They are revealing how evolution occurred in the past and will continue in the future.

The small picture

Small-scale evolutionary change is known as **microevolution**. It may take place in as little time as one generation to the next. Usually, it occurs over several generations and within a single population of plants or animals.

A classic example is the European house sparrow that was introduced to North America. It was first released in Brooklyn, New York, in the early 1850s and elsewhere (such as Galveston, Texas) between 1867 and 1872. By 1914, sparrows were found in Death Valley, California. Today, they can be found all over the continent and as far south as Costa Rica. The birds found furthest from their release point are slightly different from the ones close by. Different groups vary in colour, size, and shape. For example, sparrows in the north are generally larger than those in the southwest. This variation within the different groups has occurred during the past 150 years, across no more than about 100 generations of sparrows. It is evolution in action that scientists have been able to observe first-hand.

The big picture

Large-scale evolutionary change is known as **macroevolution**. This usually occurs above species level. It covers the great trends in evolution, such as the rise of the dinosaurs, the spread of flowering plants, or the return of whales to the ocean. Macroevolution is not easy to observe because it occurs over millions of years. It very much relies on finding **fossils** in rocks to reconstruct the history of life on Earth – all 4 billion years of it.

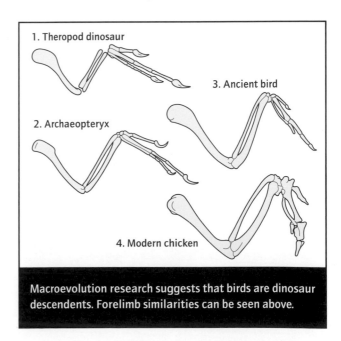

1. Theropod dinosaur
2. Archaeopteryx
3. Ancient bird
4. Modern chicken

Macroevolution research suggests that birds are dinosaur descendents. Forelimb similarities can be seen above.

Speed and direction

Evolution is not constant. It seems to go in fits and starts. Periods of gradual change are interspersed with short bursts of rapid evolution. This process is known as punctuated equilibrium. The environmental pressure on a species governs the rate of evolution. Little pressure results in slow change; while a strong pressure can be so catastrophic that the species might not cope and eventually becomes **extinct**. A species' disappearance leaves a vacant gap called a niche, so other species evolve more rapidly in the race to fill it. Certain environmental conditions accelerate evolution, too.

On reaching an island, "small" animals are not harassed by their normal **predators** and are isolated from their competitors. Some evolve rapidly into much larger animals than their mainland relatives. For example, the giant tortoises on the Galapagos Islands and the Indonesian Komodo dragon. However, the opposite generally occurs to large animals arriving on islands with less available food – they tend to evolve into smaller creatures. Fossils of dwarf elephants found on islands in the Mediterranean illustrate this point.

Virginie Millien, from McGill University, Canada, has worked out the rate of these evolutionary changes. She has found that they take place up to three times quicker on islands than on the mainland. The periods of time are as small as several thousands of years or even a few decades.

The Indonesian island of Komodo is home to the world's largest lizard, the Komodo dragon. Its main prey was a now extinct dwarf elephant. Many islands have dwarfs and giants. Large plant-eaters have limited food supplies, so small plant-eating animals generally survive better than large ones. Meat-eaters have fewer competitors, so larger meat-eating animals can survive.

Which way evolution?

While evolution can seem chaotic and unpredictable, it has a direction. The move is towards increased "fitness". The principle is simple. Fit individuals become more numerous in a population, while less fit ones tend to be scarce. For example, if there was a cooling of the climate, a hairy mammoth might evolve from a hairless elephant. The mammoth would be "fitter" to live in a cold climate.

Enter the Red Queen

In the natural world, no individual is alone. It has competitors for resources, such as food and living space, and it can be both predator or **prey**. This means that it is not evolving in isolation. Others with which it interacts have also been evolving. For example, predators and prey evolve the ability to outdo each other, the so-called "**arms race**" (see page 44). Sometimes the cheetah catches the gazelle, but sometimes the gazelle escapes. Whichever way, these two animals are continually playing catch-up. This phenomenon is known as the Red Queen Principle. The Red Queen in Lewis Carroll's book *Through the Looking-Glass* said: "Now, here, you see, it takes all the running you can do, to keep in the same place". In evolutionary terms, this means that in a competitive world an individual must progress simply to maintain its place in the **ecosystem**.

Dwarf elephants stood no more than 140 cm (55 in.) at the shoulder and weighed 200 kg (440 lb).

180cm

150cm

120cm

90cm

60cm

30cm

CHARLES DARWIN
(1809–1882)

Charles Darwin's theory of evolution is one of science's most famous theories. Intending later to become a clergyman, he joined H.M.S. *Beagle* on a voyage around the world in 1831. The extraordinary things he saw during the journey pushed him towards a life in science. Darwin kept a detailed diary and collected **specimens** that were sent back to England. He explored the rainforest in Brazil, and excavated the fossils of giant ground sloths in Patagonia. But it was in the Galapagos Islands that he gathered information that was to lead to his theory of evolution.

It was later brought to Darwin's attention that the finches on each island were slightly different. Although of a similar size and colour, their bills varied with their diet.

▲ *Each species of finch in the Galapagos Islands is adapted to exploit food that is locally abundant, and this has resulted in bills of different shapes and sizes.*

Some had robust beaks to crack seeds and others had more slender beaks to take pulp from cactus fruits. There was even a finch that drank blood and another that used cactus spines as a tool to dislodge grubs hidden under bark. Though different, all birds bore a resemblance to a single species that lived on the mainland of nearby South America.

This led Darwin to suggest that some birds from the mainland had reached the islands and their descendants had populated them. They were the common **ancestors** of all the Galapagos finches. Over many generations they had **adapted** to the conditions and foods on each island, and because they were separated, eventually each became a new species. It is a phenomenon known today as adaptive radiation.

More importantly, Darwin realised that each new species had a characteristic advantageous to its environment, in each case a modification of the bill. So, the finches adapted to eat cactus fruits obtained more food where cacti grew than those with, say, seed-eating bills. The cactus eaters were the ones that thrived, reproduced, and eventually came to dominate that particular habitat. It was a process that Darwin called **natural selection**, and it was central to his theory of evolution. Nature, he suggested, had selected the finch that would best survive – in the words of Herbert Spencer: **"survival of the fittest"**.

Darwin was not alone

Darwin was not the only scientist of his day to propose a theory of evolution. Before he was born, the French naturalist, Jean-Baptiste Lamarck (1744–1829), had proposed his theory of "inheritance of acquired traits". Lamarck thought that evolution happened when individuals adapted to environmental pressures during their lifetime, and passed these adaptations on to their offspring.

More significant were the ideas of renowned naturalist, Alfred Russel Wallace. Wallace independently came to the same conclusion as Darwin. In 1858, papers from both authors were jointly presented at the Linnean Society in London, UK. However, it was Darwin who captured the public's attention a year later when he published his famous work *On the Origin of Species*. It was a huge seller!

NATURE OF SCIENTIFIC THEORY

A theory in science is a logical explanation based on observable facts. It is not a hunch or unproven guess, as it can be in everyday speech. So it is incorrect to say "It's not fact, it's only a theory". Theory and fact are not opposites. Theories interpret facts. Darwin was very careful to gather together as many observations as he could before presenting his theory of evolution to the scientific community. After the voyage of the *Beagle* (1831–36), Darwin worked on his theory for 20 years before publishing it.

Finches were not the only creatures to ▶ *be noticed. The giant tortoises have differently shaped carapaces (shells) on different islands. The saddle-shaped shell is found on tortoises in areas of poor vegetation. As shown here, it allows them to stretch their necks to reach higher plants. The domed shell is found on tortoises feeding in more lush vegetation.*

The light and dark peppered moths occurred as a result of industrial pollution.

Evolution in action

In 1859, Charles Darwin's theory of evolution came as quite a bombshell to some members of Victorian society. He was criticised mercilessly, not least by the Church that took the words of *The Bible* quite literally. It concentrated on the view that God created all living things just once and that the Earth was no more than 6,000 years old.

One of Darwin's problems was that evolution generally takes place over millions of years, so it was difficult to show it actually happening. However, in the mill towns of industrial England, a small creature eventually changed all that. It was the peppered moth (*Biston betularia*) which was studied in the 1950s by British **ecologist** H. B. D. Kettlewell. Before the Industrial Revolution, the pale form of the moth

dominated in the north of England. However, in the mid-19th century a darker form of the peppered moth began to dominate. Why was this?

The switch was the result of industrial pollution. Soot covered any exposed surfaces, so the darker moth was better camouflaged. The lighter moth was spotted easily by bird predators and its numbers declined. During the 20th century, however, industrial pollution was reduced and soot practically disappeared. Now the dark form of the moth was more obvious and its population went into decline. In each case, nature favoured the moth that was camouflaged – survival of the fittest. So, changes in the colour of peppered moths became an observable example of natural selection, in which at least one factor influencing that change was predation by birds.

CONTROVERSIAL THEORIES

There are three main theories of life's history.

- Evolution proposes that all of life descended from a common ancestor.
- Transformism suggests that changes can occur within a line of direct descendants, but species do not go extinct, and lines do not split off to produce new species.
- Creationism, which includes "intelligent design", advocates that each species has a separate origin and never changes. Its supporters argue that there must have been an intelligent cause behind the diversity of life.

All the evidence, such as that from **palaeontology**, **genetics**, **molecular biology**, and many other scientific **disciplines**, indicates that evolution is the most likely explanation for the diversity of life on Earth. Although a theory, it is supported by much evidence, all of which comes in many forms. In molecular biology, the discovery of the structure of **DNA** (see page 31), and the revelation that the genetic code of all life forms has the same basic structure, points to a common ancestor. From palaeontology and **taxonomy** (the studies of fossils and **classification**), the succession of major groups of living things in the **fossil** record is also indicative of a common ancestor. It is like detecting a crime, with scientists discovering the many clues that come together to solve the case.

TREES OF LIFE

With such a great **diversity of species** on Earth, it should come as no surprise that scientists have attempted to bring some order to it all. They tried to group together related living things in order to create some form of **classification**. The ancient philosophers, such as Aristotle (384–322BC) with his "Great Chain of Being", envisaged a ladder with the most simple **organisms** at the bottom and the most sophisticated at the top. This implied that higher organisms are more "advanced" than lower ones, but this is not the case. In reality, all organisms living today are distantly related, and in any evolutionary ladder they all would have to be on the top rung. This is clearly impractical, so scientists turned to an evolutionary "tree" instead.

ARISTOTLE'S "GREAT CHAIN OF BEING"

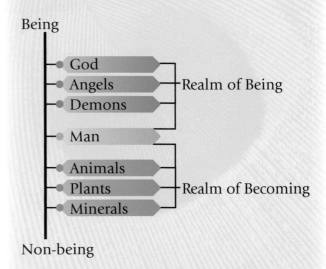

▲ *Aristotle's "Great Chain of Being" was an early attempt at classifying organisms. It includes non-living and supernatural beings as well as plants and animals.*

4TH CENTURY BC
Aristotle compiles his "Great Chain of Being".

1543
Andreas Vesalius publishes *De humani corporis fabrica* (*On the Fabric of the Human Body*).

1735
Carl Linnaeus publishes *Systema Naturae* – his first classification of living things.

| 400 BC | 1500 | 1700 |

BIRDS AND DINOSAURS

One outcome of modern classification has been the revelation that birds are in a group called a "clade" with theropod dinosaurs. The theropod dinosaurs evolved during the Jurassic period, 200–150 million years ago, from a dinosaur group that includes *Velociraptor* and *Oviraptor*. Some species of these dinosaurs had feathers and might have been capable of powered flight, using flapping wings. In fact, it has recently been proven that birds descended from dinosaurs!

Ordering life

In the past, scientists organised living things in a tree that looked just like a real tree, with branches showing different groups of organisms. They tended to group different organisms by size and shape. Today, scientists tend to build a diagram called a **cladogram** or phylogeny. This shows evolutionary relationships rather than simply comparing the size and shape of organisms. They note similarities and differences between species, and are especially interested in shared characteristics **inherited** from the common **ancestor**. The more similarities there are, the more recently two species split from a common ancestor, making them more closely related.

All sorts of characteristics can be monitored. In the early days of **taxonomy** (the study of classification), they were mostly anatomical (body) features, or stages in the development of an embryo – things relatively easy to see. The radius bone in a chimpanzee's arm, a bird's wing, and a whale's flipper is an anatomical feature. It suggests these three creatures are more closely related than, say, they are with a beetle, that has no radius and no internal skeleton. Today, we can add evidence from other **disciplines**, such as **molecular biology**, with comparisons of DNA (Deoxyribonucleic acid), RNA (Ribonucleic acid), and protein sequences. This makes information about each species even more precise and the cladogram more convincing.

CLADOGRAMS

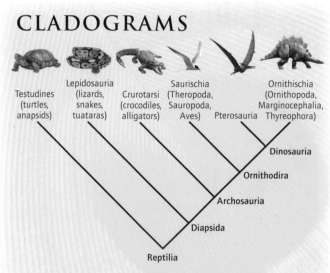

▲ A cladogram *resembles a tree with all the species or animal groups along the top where the leaves would be. Each junction (called a node) is mainly a two-way split. This shows the point at which the evolution of a new species occurred. Groups of species – the actual clades – share the same characteristics as well as an ancestor unique to them and no other group.*

1809
Jean-Baptiste Lamarck publishes *Zoological Philosophy* and a first theory of evolution based on "acquired characteristics".

1859
Darwin publishes *On the Origin of Species* – his theory of evolution based on natural selection.

1966
Willi Hennig publishes *Phylogenetic systematics* – the concept of classification now referred to as cladistics.

1800   1850   1900   **Present day**

ANDREAS VESALIUS
(1514–1564)

Andreas Vesalius, born in Brussels in 1514, was educated in Paris, France, and Padua, Italy. He was fascinated by the **anatomy** of the human body. When he was appointed the Professor of Surgery and Anatomy at the University of Padua, in 1537, he conducted all his own dissections. Lectures and demonstrations were based on the work of famous ancient Greek physician Galen, who dominated medical science at the time. Other professors simply read Galen's work aloud while a surgeon carried out the dissection. In doing his own dissections, however, Vesalius realised that Galen's accounts were wrong. Galen wrote that seven bones made up the human breastbone, while Vesalius could find only three. Galen also claimed the humerus (upper arm) was the longest bone in the body, but Vesalius saw that the femur was the longest. Why was Galen so wrong?

In 1541, whilst a guest lecturer at the University of Bologna, Vesalius realised that in Roman times Galen would have been banned from dissecting people. Galen's "human" dissections were actually of Barbary macaques (monkeys from North Africa) and oxen. Nobody had bothered to check them! Galen had thought the monkeys were similar inside to humans. But Vesalius found that there were significant differences. One is that the lower jawbone is a single bone in humans and two bones in monkeys.

Vesalius had not only shown the importance of anatomy in medicine but unknowingly had kick-started comparative anatomy (the science of comparing bodies). This kind of accurate anatomical evidence helped Darwin formulate his theory of evolution years later.

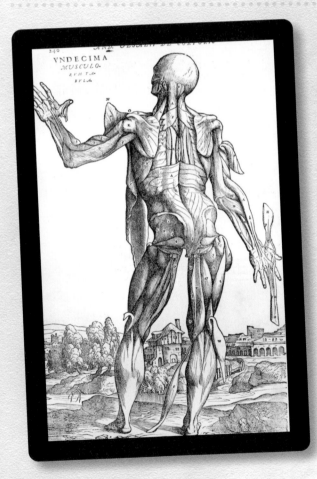

▲ *Anatomical drawings by Vesalius were the first to accurately detail the human body. Curiously, though, the skeletons and corpses were often set in "artistic" settings – against a Roman plinth or in the Italian countryside.*

Inside and out

Although Vesalius noticed the differences between humans and monkeys, his work focussed mainly on human anatomy. It was the French naturalist, Pierre Belon (1517–1564), who took it further. He wrote books on the natural history of birds, fish, and other water creatures. In these he compared the anatomy of wild animals with that of humans. He is credited with being the "father" of modern, comparative anatomy.

Homologies and analogies

Comparative anatomy is the study of the similarities and differences in the shape and structure of different organisms. It is based on two distinct concepts – homologies and analogies. Homologies are body parts that are similar in different **species**, because those species had a common ancestor. However, they may not perform the same function. The mammalian forelimb is an example. The skeleton of the wrist and hand of a monkey has the same basic structure as a bat's wing, or a dolphin's flipper. But one is for grasping, one for powered flight, and one for swimming. The more homologies shared by organisms, the more closely related they are likely to be.

Analogies are anatomical structures that are similar in appearance because they evolved in a similar environment. However, these were

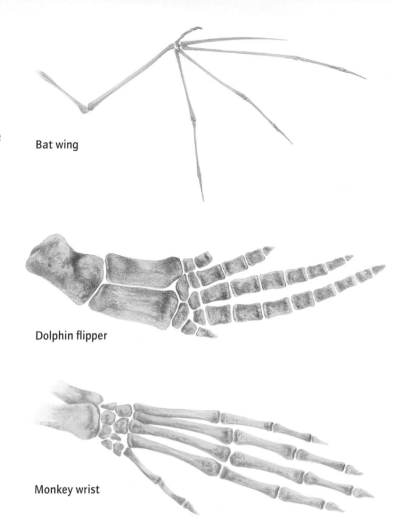

Bat wing

Dolphin flipper

Monkey wrist

The forelimbs of a bat, dolphin, and monkey have similar bones that are modified to suit different lifestyles.

not inherited from a common ancestor. The torpedo body shape and dorsal fin of sharks, ichthyosaurs, and dolphins have a similar function – they enable the creatures to swim rapidly through water. But they are derived quite separately, from very different ancestors. It is a case of convergent evolution, in which living things evolve towards a similar form.

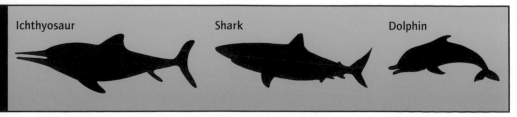

The body shapes of ichthyosaurs, sharks, and dolphins are similar even though the animals are unrelated.

Ichthyosaur

Shark

Dolphin

Convergent evolution

Animals that are totally unrelated, and living at different times or on different continents, sometimes evolve the same characteristics quite independently. This is the result of **adaptations** to similar environmental challenges. It is a phenomenon called convergent evolution. For example, it is believed that powered flight evolved four times during the Earth's history as a means of escaping **predators** or chasing **prey**.

- 300 million years ago, insects began to fly. These first miniature aeronauts were very similar to the modern stonefly (above right). When it emerges from its aquatic nymph stage, it skims over the water on primitive wings.
- Pterosaurs (below left) are flying reptiles related to dinosaurs that first flew 225 million years ago. They evolved from fast, ground-running ancestors and possibly took off at first using a "ground-up" method.

- This differed from birds (above left) that are thought to have launched themselves into the air 124 million years ago, adopting a "tree-down" approach.
- Bats (below right) appeared in the Eocene **epoch**, between 55 and 34 million years ago. They evolved from an ancient **nocturnal** insectivore that took to the air.

There are not many fossils of the ancestors of each group, so it is difficult to find evidence for explanations of the four independent origins of flight. Pterosaurs and birds may have originally taken off by running downhill or by leaping off cliffs. Whichever method they used they solved the problem of taking to the air in the same way – using wings.

Birds, stoneflies, pterosaurs, and bats solved flying in the same way – they evolved wings!

Woodpecker stand-ins

Convergent evolution is not confined to anatomy. **Behaviour** can converge, too. Look at these examples:

- Winkling out wood-boring insect larvae, with their strong bill and stiff tongue, is a special feeding technique used by European and North American woodpeckers.
- In Madagascar, where there are no woodpeckers, a nocturnal lemur called the aye-aye adopts a similar feeding technique. Instead of using a bill, it locates and extracts grubs from holes in trees using an elongated middle finger.
- The **marsupial** striped opossum in Australia has a similar modification to one of its fingers.
- In New Caledonia, a species of crow creates a tool from a thorn or sharp twig. It uses

this, like the woodpecker's bill and the aye-aye's finger, to probe and forage for grubs.

All these animals are totally unrelated, yet they have solved the same feeding problem in a similar way.

HOVERING BIRDS

In America, hummingbirds have taken powered flight to an extreme. Depending on the species, they flap their wings up to 80 times each second. They can also hover, and even fly backwards or vertically, while feeding on the nectar from flowers. The unrelated sunbirds in Africa, and the honeyeaters in Australia, have adopted the same trick. Though many perch while feeding, some smaller species can hover while sipping nectar – another case of convergent evolution.

This aye-aye has extracted a substantial meal with its elongated finger.

CARL LINNAEUS
(1707–1778)

▲ *The Swedish physician and biologist, Carl Linnaeus, was the undisputed "father of taxonomy". In 1735, he published the first edition of his book classifying living things,* Systema Naturae. *He updated it continually so that, in 1758, the tenth edition included 4,400 classified species of animals and 7,700 species of plants. He was ennobled as Carl von Linné in 1761.*

The great diversity of life on Earth not only needs classifying, but each organism also has to have a name. Naming animals is fraught with difficulties because names are not consistent in different areas. The woodlouse, for example, has 34 common names devoted to it in the English county of Devon alone. There is also the problem of confusion. In the English language, a goose barnacle is not the same as a barnacle goose, and spider crabs and crab spiders are very different. Cuttlefish and crayfish are not fish, and glow-worms and slow-worms are not worms. So each living thing needs a scientific name that can be understood by everybody in the world.

Carl Linnaeus laid the foundations for naming living organisms. He devised a simple solution, giving each organism a name in two parts, known as binomial nomenclature. The first is its **genus**, a name shared with very similar organisms. The second is a specific name, or term, unique to that species. Both words are in Latin and often help to describe the main feature of the species or its place of origin. In this way, one of the ancient human ancestors is called *Homo erectus*, which refers to "man who stands upright". People's names are often incorporated. A damaged **specimen** of a new species of long-beaked echidna was discovered in a drawer in a Dutch museum. It was named *Zaglossus attenboroughi* in honour of the television wildlife presenter, Sir David Attenborough.

The words are always written in italics. The genus name, e.g. *Homo*, always has an upper case opening letter and the species name, e.g. *erectus*, is always all lower case. Nowadays, modern words are often latinised, the genus name forming a Latin noun and the specific name an adjective.

Ordering nature

Linnaeus not only devised a naming system, he also developed a classification system. It is not as precise as the modern cladogram (see page 15) and was more for ease of naming than to show evolutionary descent. However, it is still widely used today (although it has evolved since Linnaeus first proposed it) and classifies living things in a **hierarchy**. Today, three domains – Archaea, **Bacteria**, and Eukaryota – occupy the highest level. The next level down has the kingdoms, followed by phyla, **classes**, **orders**, families, genera, and species. There may be sub-groupings of these headings, such as cohorts and divisions, as well as sub-species, varieties, races, morphs, strains, and forms, all of which appear below the species level.

Bacteria may be classified as strains by the addition of a number and letter sequence. For example, *Escherichia coli* 0157:H7 is a strain of bacterium that causes severe food poisoning in humans.

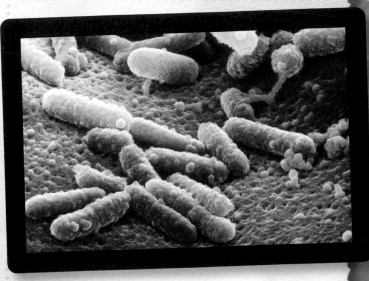

▲ Each strain of Escherichia coli *is classified with a number. Some strains are harmless gut bacteria, while others cause serious food poisoning.*

EXAMPLE OF LINNAEUS' CLASSIFICATION SYSTEM

Level	Name	Key features
Domain	Eukaryota	**Cells** with a nucleus.
Kingdom	Animalia	Cell membrane but no cell wall.
Phylum	Chordata	Notochord and pharyngeal gill slits (maybe vestigial).
Sub-phylum	Vertebrata	Backbone.
Class	Mammalia	Hair, mammary glands, and milk.
Sub-class	Placentalia	Give birth to live young after full internal gestation period.
Order	Primates	Collar bone, forward-facing eyes, grasping hands.
Family	Hominidae	Upright posture, large brain, stereo vision, flat face, hands and feet are differentiated.
Genus	*Homo*	S-shaped spine.
Species	*sapiens*	High forehead, chin, thin skull bones.

▲ *The Linnean classification of humans, from the general (top) to the more specific.*

HOW EVOLUTION WORKS

A culture of *Staphylococcus* bacteria showing a patch of penicillin-resistant bacteria on the right.

Darwin believed that the principle mechanism of evolution was **natural selection**. It is probably the single most important concept in modern biology. Natural selection is the process by which **inherited** characteristics are passed on. Positive, favourable characteristics become more common in following generations. Negative, unfavourable characteristics become less common. It means that individuals in a **population** with the favourable characteristics are the ones most likely to survive and reproduce.

1865
Austrian monk Gregor Mendel explains how the characteristics of pea plants are passed on as pairs of genes.

1903
Dutch botanist Walter Sutton links to Mendel's theories and suggests that pairs of **chromosomes** carry hereditary information.

1911
Thomas Hunt Morgan explains how genes are arranged on chromosomes.

| 1850 | 1875 | 1900 |

Super-bugs

Natural selection is evident in our everyday lives, in the development of antibiotic resistance in disease-causing **bacteria**. **Penicillin** was discovered in 1928, by the Scottish biologist Alexander Fleming, at St. Mary's Hospital in London, UK. He noticed a mould killing the bacteria in his bacterial cultures. The mould was called *Penicillium*. Later, scientists Ernst Chain and Howard Florey isolated and extracted penicillin. It became the main weapon in the fight against bacterial diseases.

Though most bacteria are killed when exposed to penicillin, a few survive. The survivors often have **enzymes** that deactivate the antibiotic, making it powerless. This deactivation ability is inherited. So, when the bacterium's offspring are confronted with the antibiotic they, too, survive. Eventually, the entire population of that bacteria becomes immune. But how does this affect us?

In recent years, natural selection in bacterial populations has had a devastating effect in hospitals. The widespread and sometimes inappropriate use of antibiotics, such as for treating virus-caused diseases like colds or flu, has meant that resistance to antibiotics has increased. This has produced "super-bugs", such as MRSA (methicillin-resistant *Staphylococcus aureus*). The speed with which resistance occurs is scary. In the 1990s, a new **class** of antibiotics, linezolid, was effective against MRSA. In 2003, the first case of linezolid-resistance was recorded.

Different antibiotics continue to be directed at MRSA. But in this escalating **arms race** between the bacterium and antibiotics researchers, the bacterium is currently winning.

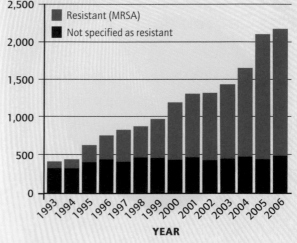

DEATHS RELATED TO MRSA, 1993–2006

▲ *This graph shows the number of deaths related to MRSA in England and Wales. The number increased substantially from 1996–2005, but stabilised in 2006.*

1944
Oswald Avery, Colin Macleod, and Maclyn McCarty confirm that DNA is the **molecule** carrying hereditary information.

1951
English biophysicist Rosalind Franklin's X-ray pictures show DNA to be a helix.

1953
Francis Crick and James Watson unravel the structure of DNA.

1925   1950   1975

Wilson's bird-of-paradise is an extremely elaborate figure, from its gleaming blue head to its ornately curled, silver tail feathers.

Pests get the upper hand

Natural selection is also evident in pesticide resistance in agriculture, medicine, and in the home. When pests develop a resistance to a pesticide, they reproduce unchecked. In some areas, populations of malaria-carrying mosquitoes have developed a resistance to a chemical called DDT (Dichloro-Diphenyl-Trichloroethane), one of the main weapons against them. The disease is on the increase again, killing over two million people each year. Around 1980, in towns and cities in the UK, rats developed a resistance to the pesticide warfarin and their numbers increased. In orange groves in the USA, fruit flies are resistant to malathion, the pesticide normally used to control them. Ironically, US farmers lost about seven percent of their crops to pests in the 1940s before pesticides were used routinely. Now they lose 13 percent, yet more pesticides are being used.

Impressive rituals

Natural selection can be the result of sexual selection – a choice of partner made by individual, living **organisms**. Sexual selection takes many forms. Males of the **species** tend to fight for the right to mate or impress the females with some form of elaborate display. The fighters have "weapons", such as horns, while the singers and dancers have "ornaments", such as brightly coloured feathers. Both of these methods have led to extravagant and sometimes bizarre combat or courtship rituals. In many cases, it has led to a striking difference in colour, shape, and size between males and females. This phenomenon is known as sexual dimorphism.

Singers and dancers

The female of the species chooses her partner by how well he demonstrates his **prowess** or skills. Male prairie chickens strut their stuff; peacocks display their eye-catching tail; manakins perform loop-the-loop dances; bowerbirds build magnificent avenues and maypoles. But the most exotic performances are reserved for New Guinea's birds-of-paradise. Wilson's bird-of-paradise is adorned by one of the most elegant uniforms. It is mainly red and black, with a green breast, a yellow mantle on its neck, blue feet, and naked blue skin on the top of its head. But how can an animal afford such extravagance?

Birds-of-paradise, and many other exotic birds, live in rainforests. Here, food is plentiful and threats are few. Free of other pressures, the males of each species were free to develop their brightly coloured feather patterns

FEMALE CHOICE

Despite all the competition between males, it is usually the female that chooses who will father her offspring. The female produces eggs, and it is she who has some degree of control over whose sperm fertilises them. Scientists believe a female's choice is based on several qualities:

- Healthy male – a male's appearance and performance may indicate it is healthy, with few parasites.
- Good **genes** – the healthy-looking male is likely to pass on good genes that will enable offspring to survive.

- Runaway selection – females prefer partners who are sexually attractive. This increases the chances of their offspring being sexually attractive and, therefore, more likely to reproduce.

Why a female chooses a particular mate could be any one, or a combination, of these qualities.

and elaborate dances in order to attract a mate. These birds have focussed on making themselves more attractive in sexual **competition**. Any trait or feature that made a bird more attractive was passed on to following generations. It is the sexual equivalent of Darwin's finches. Except, in this environment, survival is less important than impressing a female and mating successfully.

Fighters

Both deer and beetle stags have elaborate antlers to engage in head-to-head combat, and bull elephants often decide on a winner by which elephant has the longest and strongest tusks. But the most extreme feature of recent times must have been that of the Irish, or giant, elk. The largest deer that ever lived – the stag was about 2.1 m (7 ft.) tall at the shoulders – it also had the largest set of antlers of any deer, up to 3.65 m (12 ft.)

across. Why it became **extinct** about 7,000 years ago is still a mystery. It could have been because people hunted it out of existence, but nobody actually knows.

The vast antlers of this now extinct giant elk provide a majestic profile, not to mention an impressively hefty weapon.

Chance in evolution

Natural selection is not the only major mechanism of evolutionary change. "Luck" can also play a part in the form of genetic drift. While natural selection produces **adaptations** that help following generations to survive and reproduce, genetic drift is completely random. It can affect the genetic make-up of a population (usually a small rather than large population) strictly by chance. The result is that the new **generation** is born with a different share of traits than the previous generation. Unlike natural selection, with genetic drift there is no guarantee that the new generation will be fitter. How does genetic drift occur?

"Chance" events, natural or caused by humans, such as earthquakes, floods, forest fires, diseases, hunting, pollution, or war can knockout a large chunk of a population. The genes of survivors then dominate that population. This is not a position that has been "won" through natural selection but gained purely through luck. If fresh genes from outside the population are not to hand it can lead to inbreeding. This results in a population of less fit individuals.

Genetic bottleneck

During the 19th century, the northern elephant seal on the west coast of North America was hunted almost to the point of **extinction**. Hunting was the "chance" event.

Two bull elephant seals square-off for a fight! They are not very different genetically, which makes the entire population susceptible to disease rather than just a few individuals.

Old Order Amish people live in closed communities, marrying amongst themselves. They have been using horses for farming and transport since they arrived in America in the early 18th century.

By 1890, only about 20 individuals survived. Their survival wasn't due to them being any fitter than the rest, they were simply lucky not to be shot. Today, the seal population is near 30,000 but their genetic variation is low. This means that the whole population is more vulnerable to the affects of disease or natural disasters, such as global warming. This extreme form of inbreeding is known as a "genetic bottleneck". It shows how genetic drift does not lose its effect even when the population increases. Darwin was unaware of genetic drift. Yet it is probably just as important as natural selection in the evolution of life on Earth.

THE "FOUNDER EFFECT"

An extreme type of genetic drift is the "founder effect". If a population emigrates to a new place, or is significantly reduced in size because of environmental change, a new population group is formed. The genes of the "founders" of this new population then appear more frequently in following generations. The Old Order Amish people, who live in Lancaster County in Pennsylvania, USA, illustrate this point. In the 18th century, just 200 Amish arrived from southwest Germany to start their new life in North America. The community is tight-knit so they marry amongst themselves. The consequence is that **recessive** genes are expressed more often. So the Amish tend to carry genetic **mutations** that are rare in the population at large. One is a form of dwarfism that is accompanied by extra fingers or toes. This can be traced back to one couple, "the founders" – Samuel King and his wife – who emigrated to the USA in 1744.

GREGOR MENDEL
(1822–1884)

Gregor Johann Mendel was born in Austria. He lived at the same time as Darwin, but the pair did not collaborate. Mendel was an Augustinian monk who showed an interest in variation in plants. He carried out experiments in the monastery gardens. If he found a plant to be slightly different from normal he would plant it alongside a "normal" one. By doing this, he found that the daughter plants of the two neighbours had some of the same characteristics or traits as the parent plants. He was beginning to unlock the secrets of **heredity**.

Mendel then began to crossbreed plants with different features to see what the outcome might be. His experimental subjects were peas. Between 1856 and 1863, he undertook an intensive cultivation programme, to closely watch the fate of seven key traits in parent and daughter pea plants. He discovered that inherited traits, such as flower colour or seed wrinkles, are not combined in the offspring, but passed intact, half from one parent and half from the other. He then realised that certain traits are "dominant" over traits that are less dominant, which are known as "recessive" traits. These traits appear in certain numerical ratios, or proportions. It means that different offspring from the same parents receive different combinations of traits. One in four had dominant traits, two had a mixture, and one showed recessive traits.

Mendel's work inspired the laws of heredity and laid foundations for modern **genetics**. But the importance of his work was not appreciated until the next century. After his pea experiments, Mendel studied bees in an attempt to extend his work to animals. He successfully produced hybrid bees that were especially good at producing honey. However, they were so vicious they had to be destroyed!

MENDEL'S PEA BREEDING RESULTS

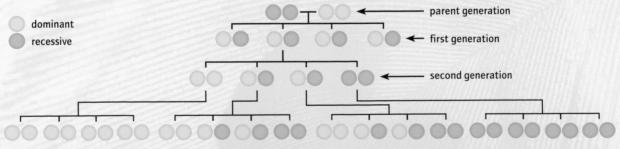

▲ *Diagram of results from Mendel's pea experiments, showing the ratio of dominant to recessive genes.*

Packs of feral dogs (domestic dogs gone wild), including breeds ranging from poodles to German shepherds, are interbreeding with wild wolves in Italy's Abruzzo Mountains. The result is that the wolf stock is not pure anymore and the Italian wolf could become extinct.

Genes on the move

In nature, the characteristics or traits from one population can be introduced into another by interbreeding. This is known as gene flow, or gene migration. Examples are pollen being blown to a new place or people moving to a new country. The frequency of this happening depends on how mobile an organism is. Generally, animals are more mobile than plants. The greater the exchange of genes between populations of the same species, the less likely it is that new species will emerge. On the other hand, a smaller flow, or no flow at all, could give rise to new species.

Barriers that affect gene flow include oceans, deserts, and mountain ranges. There is even evidence that man-made structures have disrupted gene flow. For example, plant species on one side of the Great Wall of China are genetically different from those of the same species on the other side. Here, the wall has formed a barrier against wind pollination and seed dispersal.

Gene pollution

Gene flow can also give rise to genetic pollution. In the debate about GM (genetically modified) crops, gene flow via airborne or insect-carried pollen is an issue. Some crops are genetically engineered to be resistant to insects or tolerant of herbicides. The concern is that genes from such crops could end up in the neighbouring wild population, creating "superweeds" that are difficult, if not impossible, to control. Abandoned, domesticated animals returning to a wild way of life pose a similar problem. The wild wolves of the Abruzzo National Park, Italy, are crossbreeding with feral dogs, weakening the pure wolf stock.

Mutations

Mutations are random changes in the genes. The changes can be caused by incorrect copying during **cell** division or by exposure to ultraviolet light, radioactivity, chemicals, or viruses. Some mutations are passed on to the next generation and others are not. Mutations that disadvantage organisms eventually disappear from the population, because any organism possessing the mutation dies out. Advantageous mutations pass on to following generations, and better equip them for survival. For example, a mutation in a butterfly or moth might change the colour of its wings, making it harder to spot by **predators**. Butterflies or moths with this mutation then stand a better chance of survival and dominate the population.Those without the mutation disappear. It was a mutation that produced the darker form of the peppered moth (see page 12). This was an advantageous mutation, at least for a short time.

In some cases, mutations give rise to new species. This occurred in the laboratory of Columbia University biologist, Thomas Hunt Morgan (1866–1945). He was breeding fruit

The eyespot on this butterfly acts as a warning sign to help protect it from predators.

flies, which normally have red eyes. One day, a white-eyed fruit fly appeared – the result of a mutation. But does mutation affect us?

Mutations and people

In humans, most mutations are harmless. Most harmful ones are repaired automatically by a cell's own **DNA** repair system. However, occasionally some harmful mutations occur that result in genetic disorders. These can give rise to inherited diseases, such as hemochromatosis, where a person's intestines absorb too much iron. Mutations can also have unexpected effects. There are about 10 percent of people living in Europe who carry a mutant gene that gives them immunity to HIV (human immunodeficiency virus) infections and AIDS (acquired immunodeficiency syndrome). It is thought the mutation spread when their **ancestors** survived deadly diseases of the past, such as smallpox or the Black Death.

This leopard is melanistic. A mutation caused it to have dark fur. However, if you look closely, the normal pattern of spots is still visible.

CRICK AND WATSON

▲ *This picture shows Francis Crick and James Watson with their revolutionary DNA model.*

In early March, 1953, Francis Crick walked into his local pub in Cambridge, England, and announced: "We have found the secret of life". The "we" were British physicist Crick and US ornithologist-come-virologist, James Watson. They had worked out the double-stranded structure of DNA (deoxyribonucleic acid) – the blueprint of life. DNA is the stuff of which genes are made. It takes the form of a double **helix** that looks like a twisting ladder. On the ladder are pairs of chemicals. These are called bases. They can be unzipped during cell division to make a template against which another double helix could be made. The four bases are: adenine, thymine, guanine, and cytosine.

The DNA can reproduce itself without changing its structure, except for copying mistakes or mutations. Crick and Watson had discovered the copying mechanism for the genetic material in the nucleus, the so-called "stuff of life", and the biochemical basis for the evolution of all life on Earth.

Unravelling the structure of DNA was one of the most important scientific breakthroughs of the 20th century. It has led to many exciting developments, especially for medicine.

- A technique called gene mapping is leading to an understanding of inherited diseases by identifying the genes responsible.
- Recombinant DNA technology has made it possible to manufacture human proteins, such as insulin, to treat diseases.
- Observing the genetic profile of genes involved in cancers has helped find more effective treatments.
- DNA fingerprinting has revolutionised forensic science, helping to recognize criminals, clear the innocent, and identify the victims of serious accidents.

James Watson himself has been leading the international teams tackling the ongoing Human Genome Project. The project is currently studying the genetic content of human DNA, in an attempt to identify all 20,000–25,000 genes and uncover the three billion chemical base pairs.

ADAPTATIONS

Over a period of time, **natural selection** gives rise to **adaptations** or adjustments that equip an **organism** to live in a particular ecological place. Such adaptations can help an organism to: find and catch food; breathe air; cope with specific weather conditions; defend itself against enemies; communicate with others; reproduce. Adaptations can be **structural**, physiological, or **behavioural** and they can lead to the creation of new **species**.

Structures

Structural adaptations are often physical traits that play specific roles for the creatures that embody them.

- A polar bear's thick fur and blubber are adaptations that help it keep warm, whereas an elephant's outsize ears help it to keep cool.
- The cheetah's flexible spine and paws resembling spiked running shoes are adaptations to help it catch fast-running **prey**. While the gazelle's long, thin – yet muscular – legs enable it to quickly get away.
- The chameleon's long, sticky tongue can shoot out in the blink of an eye. This adaptation enables the creature to catch prey that would otherwise have time to fly away.

65 MYA
First primates were eating mainly insects.

50 MYA
Later primates were eating fruit and insects.

7 MYA
Apes were eating fruit and occasional meat from forest.

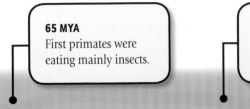

| 65 MYA | 50 MYA | 10 MYA |

MYA = million years ago

- The aquatic fly larva's "snorkel" has adapted so it can breathe underwater.
- A hedgehog's sharp spines protect it from most **predators**.

Bright colours

The most startling structural adaptations involve colour. Many butterflies have eyespots on the topside of their wings (see page 30). If threatened, they open their wings and the attacker is frightened away by the face that appears before them. Red, yellow, and black are warning colours. They indicate that the wearer is venomous, poisonous, or tastes bad – as do the black and yellow stripes of wasps and hornets. Some creatures, including hoverflies and moths, even mimic or copy more dangerous ones in an attempt to protect themselves.

Visual mimicry

Adaptation can involve a change in the entire body. Some flies, bugs, beetles, and many spiders mimic ants. This allows them to get amongst the ants for protection or to hunt them. Some are such good mimics it is hard to tell them from the real thing. There is even a mite that takes on the form of the ant's leg to which it clings! Why can't such animals spot a mimic?

Chemical mimicry

Visual mimicry may be obvious to us. but animals often use smells and sounds we find hard to detect. One species of spider lives with aggressive weaver ants. It mimics itself to look like the ants and uses chemical mimicry to smell like them and be accepted into the colony.

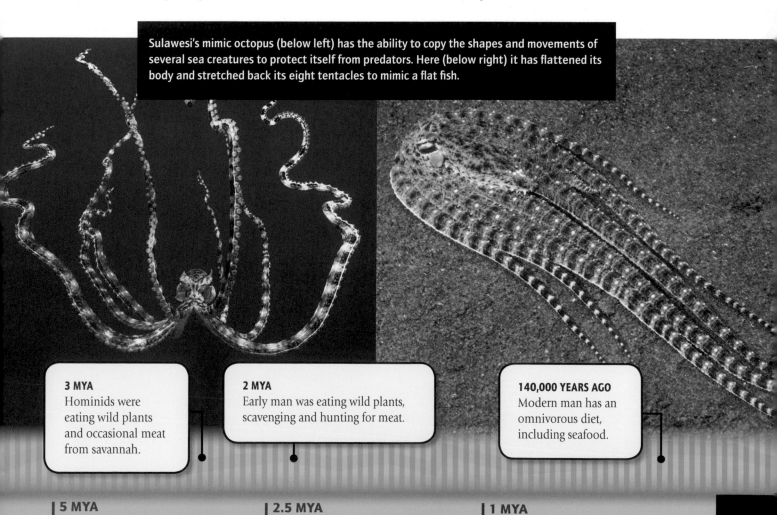

Sulawesi's mimic octopus (below left) has the ability to copy the shapes and movements of several sea creatures to protect itself from predators. Here (below right) it has flattened its body and stretched back its eight tentacles to mimic a flat fish.

3 MYA
Hominids were eating wild plants and occasional meat from savannah.

2 MYA
Early man was eating wild plants, scavenging and hunting for meat.

140,000 YEARS AGO
Modern man has an omnivorous diet, including seafood.

| 5 MYA | 2.5 MYA | 1 MYA |

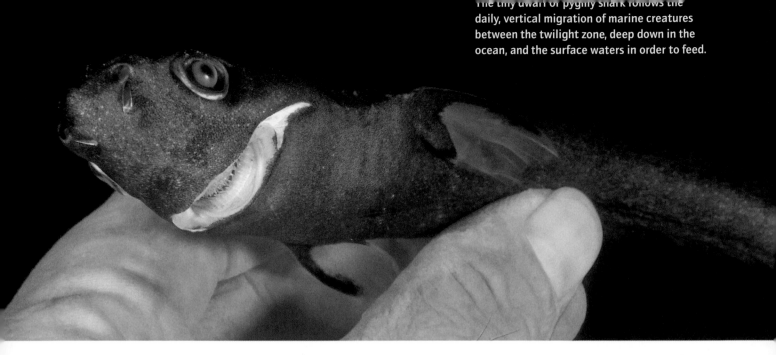

Large blue butterflies also use various guises to grow in red ant's nests. The caterpillar disguises itself with ant smells and produces a sugar solution that calms the ants. The pupating caterpillar vibrates its chrysalis at the same frequency the ants use to communicate. The ants are tricked into looking after the butterfly's caterpillar and not attacking it. It is brought up in a safe place with plenty of food: it eats the ants!

Camouflage

Camouflage is another form of visual mimicry. In the open ocean, sharks are coloured blue-grey on top and white below. Seen from below, they blend in with the bright surface waters. From above, they look a similar colour to the dark sea. Many seabirds, such as gulls, have a similar colouration. In the deep sea, where there is very little light, fish have light-emitting organs along their belly which help camouflage them against the slight glow from above.

Adaptation and behaviour

Behavioural adaptations give an organism a special way of behaving to help it survive and reproduce. Bird song is an obvious example of behavioural adaptation. Male birds perform long, repetitive vocals to warn other males off their territory or to attract females to mate. Bird song has evolved through sexual selection. It is a clear indicator of the fitness of the singer. However, the longest songs in nature are not those of birds, but the reverberating moans and whines of the humpback whale. One song can be up to 20 minutes long and can be sung over and over again for many hours! The song changes over time, but all bull (male) whales in a single **population** keep up with the changes and sing exactly the same song. Unlike with birds, female whales appear to ignore the bull's songs. So exactly why they sing is a mystery.

Long journeys

Behaviour can be extreme. One way to be in the right place at the right time is to migrate. Some species cross the entire globe to maximise their food supply, clocking up thousands of miles.

- Humpback whales travel over 8,300 km (5,157 miles) from Costa Rican breeding grounds to feeding grounds in the Antarctic.
- Grey whales commute between Baja California and the Bering Sea, off Alaska.
- Arctic terns fly to and from the Arctic and Antarctic.
- Sooty shearwaters follow a figure-of-eight track across the Pacific Ocean, covering 65,000 km (40,389 miles) each year.

Migrations are not always horizontal around the globe; some are vertical. Each night, millions of marine creatures swim up from the twilight zone, in the deep ocean, to feed in the food-rich surface waters. At daylight, they return to the depths. In this way, they maximise feeding while minimising exposure to predators. However, some predators follow the vertical migration. Tiny, deep-sea sharks, no longer than a human hand, travel 1,000 m (3,300 ft.) or more at dawn and dusk. That is the equivalent of a human running a marathon before breakfast and bedtime every day!

The sooty shearwater is the first bird to have been tracked throughout its annual migration. It arrives at key feeding sites when food is seasonally abundant, diving for fish, squid, and krill to depths of 68 m (225 ft.).

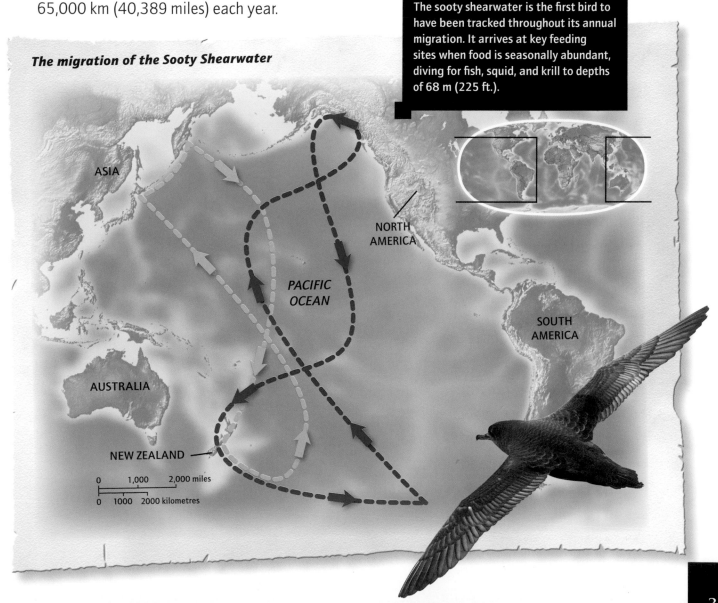

The migration of the Sooty Shearwater

ASIA

NORTH AMERICA

PACIFIC OCEAN

SOUTH AMERICA

AUSTRALIA

NEW ZEALAND

0   1,000   2,000 miles

0   1000   2000 kilometres

The bombardier beetle squirts a boiling hot cocktail of chemicals from its rear end as a form of defence. The stream is not continuous but pulsed, like machine gun fire.

Adaptation and function

Physiological adaptations are systems or processes that enable an organism to function in a particular environment. For example, rattlesnakes create venom to kill prey; slugs secrete slime in order to move; moths vibrate their wing muscles to warm up before flying.

A most unusual physiological adaptation is the defence mechanism of the bombardier beetle. Two chemicals – hydroquinone and hydrogen peroxide – mix in a chamber at the rear of the beetle's abdomen. This mixture causes an explosion and forms a boiling hot spray. The beetle swivels its abdomen at an aggressor, such as an ant or a toad, to spray it.

PHYSIOLOGY VERSUS BEHAVIOUR

Diving birds, such as cormorants, have structural and physiological adaptations to catch their food underwater. Their webbed feet are at the rear of their body for better propulsion, and they are able to dive for up to four minutes at a time. Recent research in Greenland and Normandy, France, has also revealed behavioural adaptations. In Greenland, the water temperature is a chilly 5°C (41°F) compared with an average 12°C (54°F) in Normandy. Greenland birds spend 70 percent less time in the water than Normandy birds. Yet prey capture rates are 150 percent higher in Greenland birds. Faced with the colder conditions, the Greenland birds make sure every dive counts. They spend less time at the surface of the water between dives and return to land between intensive feeding sessions.

Hibernation and aestivation

Surviving certain weather conditions can be helped by drastic physiological adaptations. In cold conditions some creatures, such as bats and ground squirrels, hibernate. Their body temperature, breathing pace, and heart rate lower. The squirrel's body temperature can drop to 2˚C (36˚F).

In hot, dry countries, desert animals behave similarly when temperatures soar, food is scarce, and water supplies are low. This is known as aestivation. One amazing aestivator is Australia's water-holding frog. Most of its life is spent in an underground burrow. During the driest spells, it secretes a mucous to form a membrane around itself and a lining to the burrow. This hardens to retain water. The frog stores this water in its bladder and pockets under its skin. Come the rain, it tears open its mucous cocoon and goes in search of a mate.

A rattlesnake can go for weeks or even months without food, allowing it to survive in the harsh conditions of the desert.

LAMARCK, DARWIN, AND ADAPTATION

Both Lamarck and Darwin (see pages 10–11) used evidence of adaptation to support their theories of evolution. But there is a fundamental difference between the two. This is illustrated by the giraffe's long neck.

Lamarck suggested that giraffes got their long necks by stretching up to reach increasingly higher leaves. He felt that, in a giraffe's lifetime, its neck got a bit longer and this characteristic was passed on to its offspring. Darwin, on the other hand, suggested that in any population some giraffe's necks would be long and others short. He felt that giraffes with longer necks survived to reproduce, while giraffes with shorter necks were at a disadvantage and

eventually died out. In Lamarck's version the long neck adaptation took place in a single **generation**. Darwin's hypothesis suggested it would take many generations to adapt. Modern **genetics** indicate that Darwin was right because information flows only from the **genes** to the processes that enable the body to work, not the other way round.

This idea also applies to acclimatisation. A person climbing Mount Everest can become acclimatised to surviving at high altitude where there is less oxygen in the air. Acclimatisation itself is not an adaptation. However, the ability to acclimatise is. Some people are able to acclimatise more quickly than others.

SPECIES
SPECIFICS

A **species** is a group of **organisms** that can reproduce together. For example, a tiger shark can successfully breed with another tiger shark but not with a hammerhead shark. A new species often arises when a **population** becomes isolated. It could be a physical barrier (such as a mountain range or island) or a social barrier (such as a change of **behaviour**). Examples of this can be seen on the isolated islands in the Galapagos Archipelago. Distinct species of finch have evolved to take advantage of food supplies local to each island. Each new population is exposed to different **natural selection** pressures or undergoes random genetic drift.

Therefore, new traits are acquired and passed down to following generations. Eventually, the two populations become so different they cannot exchange **genes** and reproduce. Thus, a new species is born.

Time shift

An example of the evolution of a new species in action is the apple maggot fly. The fly is native to North America and normally infests hawthorn fruits. In the early 19th century, settlers began growing apples and one section of the apple maggot fly population made the most of this new food source.

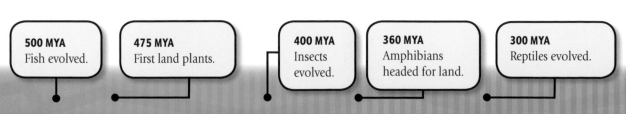

500 MYA
Fish evolved.

475 MYA
First land plants.

400 MYA
Insects evolved.

360 MYA
Amphibians headed for land.

300 MYA
Reptiles evolved.

| 500 MYA | 400 MYA | 300 MYA |

MYA = million years ago

CARIBBEAN IGUANAS

In the summer of 1995, Hurricane Marilyn ploughed through the Caribbean. Trees were uprooted and some fell into the sea. They drifted in the ocean currents to neighbouring islands, but they were not alone. The uprooted trees acted as a raft to passengers. At least 15 common iguanas are known to have rafted to the island of Anguilla, where the species was previously unknown. Scientists are now watching these animals very carefully to see if being separated from their parent stock on other islands will change the iguanas in any way. Conditions there are right for us to witness the birth of a new species.

Apples and haws grow at different times of the year. So, today, the adult flies emerge from the fruits at different times of the year and do not mix. Those emerging from apples only mate with other flies from apple trees, and those from haws only mate with other flies from hawthorn trees. As adult flies prefer to lay their eggs in the tree of their birth the populations remain segregated over generations. At the moment there do not appear to be any physical barriers to mating between the two populations of flies. Scientists believe this could be the early stages of speciation.

The spread of apple maggot flies to other members of the Rosaseae **family** of fruit trees, such as cherries, pears, and roses, means we could also be watching adaptive radiation in action. Thus, the fast formation of distinct species of a single species group to fill several ecological needs.

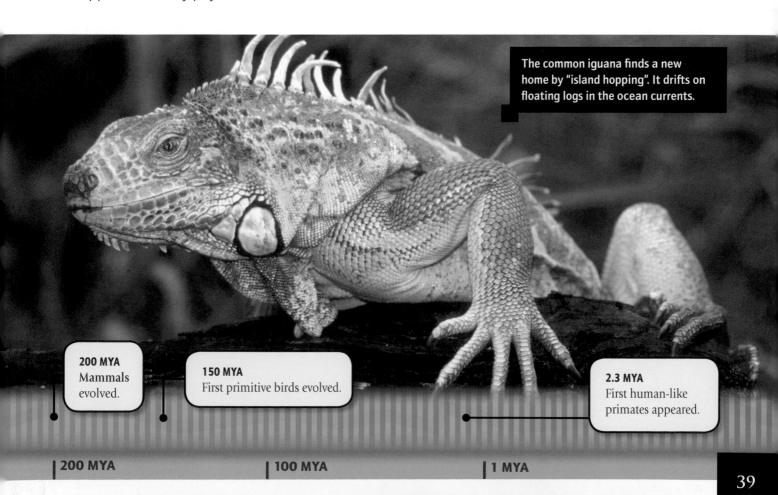

The common iguana finds a new home by "island hopping". It drifts on floating logs in the ocean currents.

200 MYA Mammals evolved.

150 MYA First primitive birds evolved.

2.3 MYA First human-like primates appeared.

200 MYA   **100 MYA**   **1 MYA**

Still living together

Sometimes species stray from each other even though they live in the same place. On the northwest coast of North America, at least two (possibly three) types of orcas or killer whales live in the same area. But they do not mix or breed together. Their feeding habits vary considerably. Resident pods (groups) feed on salmon. Transient pods eat seals and sea lions. A third transient type of smaller killer whale runs down baleen whales and their calves. Currently described as the same species, researchers are debating whether these orcas should be considered as separate species.

Co-evolution

At the beginning of the 19th century, the French aristocrat Louis-Marie Aubert du Petit-Thouars was in exile in Madagascar. He collected and described the comet orchid, a beautiful white flower with its nectar store at the end of an unusually long, whip-shaped tube, up to 30 cm- (12 in-) long. When Darwin saw it, he suggested that an insect with an extremely long proboscis or nose must pollinate it. Darwin received much scorn for his prediction, but in 1856, the Morgan's sphinx moth was found. It had a 25 cm- (10 in-) long proboscis. Unfortunately, it was in southern Africa rather than Madagascar, so the mystery of the comet orchid remained unsolved.

Alfred Russel Wallace joined the debate, publishing a drawing of what it was thought the mystery beast should look like. He was also ridiculed. However, about 21 years after Darwin's death, a subspecies of the Morgan's sphinx moth was discovered in Madagascar. It had an exceptionally long proboscis, just as Darwin had predicted. This was a case of co-evolution. Each organism is applying selection pressures on the other, to the extent that the two organisms have come to depend on each other. The flower's nectary has become so deep no other insects can reach it.

The sphinx moth has an unusually long proboscis to reach the nectaries deep in an orchid flower. The moth and the flower co-evolved, so now each is dependent on the other.

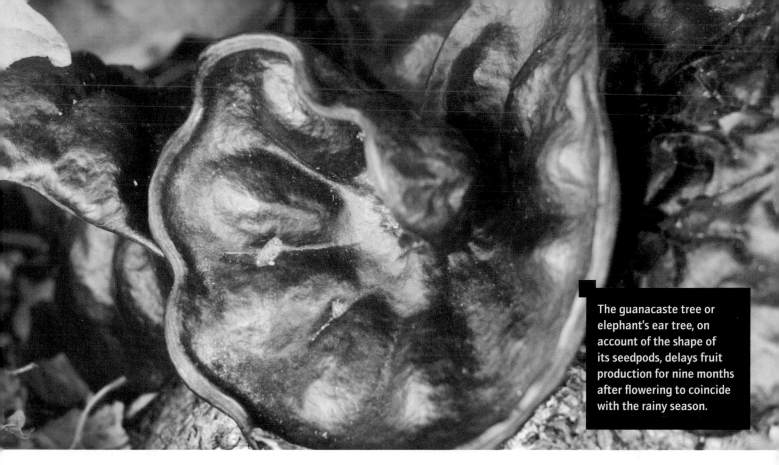

Close relationships

The close relationship between insects and flowering plants for pollination is readily observable. Other services supplied by animals, such as seed dispersal, may be less obvious.

In Costa Rica, bees help pollinate the flowers of the guanacaste tree. Its seedpods pile up below the tree and are not eaten by any native animals. This led evolutionary **ecologist** Dan Janzen, of the University of Pennsylvania, USA, to wonder how its seeds were distributed. The seed coats are extremely tough, almost like stones, and need to be cracked for water to reach the embryo. Janzen saw no sign of modern-day animals distributing the seeds by eating them, so turned to **extinct** animals for an explanation.

At one time, Costa Rica's deciduous forests were home to giant ground sloths and giant bison. Janzen believes that they ate the pods and the chewing and digestive processes scarred the fruits. This enabled them to germinate when they were dumped, together with a dollop of fertiliser, away from the parent tree. Today, domestic horses are the dispersers.

Paid ant guards

Insects supply a protection service to trees, and the trees encourage them. Azteca ants live in special compartments in the hollow stems of umbrella trees in the Amazon rainforest. They rid the tree of foliage-eating caterpillars and also snip off any vines climbing its trunk or branches. In return, the ants feed from special brown patches under the leaf stem that secrete high-energy oils and glycogen. The benefits are mutual. The tree is protected and the ants have a safe home and a ready food supply.

Forest termites are lured to their death by a ring of white, hair-like growths around the slippery rim of the pitcher of *Nepenthes albomarginata*. The pitcher is a modified leaf.

One-sided relationships

Co-evolution does not necessarily mean mutual dependence. On the island of Borneo, there is a pitcher plant, known locally as the monkey's rice pot. It is fussy about what it eats. Like all pitcher plants, its leaves form deep, pitcher-shaped containers. These pitchers are filled with water containing digestive **enzymes**. In most pitcher plants, a variety of insects fall into the pitcher, are digested, and the nutrients absorbed by the plant. But the monkey's rice pot only attracts termites. It has a line of white, hair-like structures around the top of its pitcher that are irresistible to hungry termites. The termites arrive in their hundreds and, as they feed, slip and fall into the pitcher. After an hour, all the hairs are gone, and any surviving termites scatter, leaving the plant with a pitcher full of food. Here, the plant depends on the termites, but the termites are not dependent on the plant. The white hairs are just one food source amongst many for the termites. However, the plant evolved alongside the termites and is now dependent on them for most of its food.

Parasites

One of the most common relationships on the planet is an ultimate example of one-sided co-evolution. That is the relationship between a parasite and its host. Almost every living thing is parasitized at some point in its life. A parasite has two strategies: it either reproduces slowly in or on a long-living host, or rapidly replicating parasites blitz the host and overrun it to death. Some of the relationships are quite bizarre and involve more than one host.

The tentacles of this amber snail are swollen by a parasite that forces the snail to mimic a caterpillar.

In Europe and North America, the parasitic flatworm *Leucochloridium paradoxum* has co-evolved with a bird and a snail. The flatworm lives in the bird's gut. Its eggs pass out with the bird's droppings and fall onto vegetation. Without realising it, the snail then gobbles up the eggs as it feeds. Once inside the snail, the parasite eggs change to an intermediate or midway form called miracidia. These grow into lengthened sacs that push into the snail's tentacles. Inside the sacs grow hundreds of the next stage parasite, the tailed, motile cercariae.

This impacts on the snail's life in two ways. Firstly, the snail's natural desire to seek dark and dank places is reversed, and it heads for the tops of trees. Secondly, the swollen tentacle pulsates red, green, and yellow, giving it the appearance of a newly hatched caterpillar. This attracts birds that peck at the tentacles. The snail cannot pull its tentacles into its shell to protect them because they are swollen.

This is an example of aggressive mimicry. The parasite takes on the form of the bird's natural food. But instead of a juicy caterpillar, the bird receives a mouthful of the flatworm's cercariae. These go down into the birds gut and the parasitic cycle starts all over again.

The strange, stiff-legged, leaping action shown by antelope and gazelle is called "stotting". It is an indication of how fit they are and, therefore, harder to catch.

Predators and prey

The co-evolution of **predators** and **prey** has played a big role in shaping the diversity of life on Earth. It is often an escalating **arms race**. Predators evolved claws, teeth, acute senses, and the ability to move quickly. While the prey counteract with camouflage, deadly defensive chemicals, and the ability to move faster than the predator to get away. Sometimes one is ahead of the game, sometimes the other. They even communicate. For example, antelope "stot" with stiff-legged leaps to tell a predatory cat it is too fit to be caught. And wildebeest can tell whether a lion is hunting or not simply by the way it walks.

Squirrel talk

In southwest California, USA, ground squirrels and rattlesnakes have been enemies for millions of years. As a result, the adult squirrels have evolved blood proteins that give them limited immunity to rattlesnake venom. Squirrel pups do not yet have these blood proteins, so are more vulnerable to rattlesnake attacks. However, the squirrels are more than a match for rattlesnakes. If they spot a rattlesnake trying to sneak into a nesting burrow, they repeatedly dash in to within striking range, nip the snake's tail, and throw dirt. They also wag their bushy tails back-and-forth in a behaviour known as "flagging". There is more to flagging than immediately meets the eye.

"ROBO-SQUIRREL"

Aaron Rundus has been studying tail flagging. He built a robotic squirrel, controlled by a computer, to better understand what was going on. He tested it on a rattlesnake and found that the more the squirrel flagged, the more alert the rattlesnake became and the more it rattled. The snake's behaviour had changed from predatory to defensive. In a way, the two creatures were talking to each other in a language of flagging and rattling. But that was not all.

Rundus also discovered that when confronted with a rattlesnake, the squirrel pumped more warm blood into its tail. This made its infrared, or heat signature, stronger. Rattlesnakes have special, heat-sensitive, facial pits on their snout that detect infrared. It is how they "see" their warm-blooded prey in the dark. The squirrels do not warm up their tails in response to other species of snakes (such as gopher snakes) that do not have facial pits. Why they do so to rattlesnakes is still unknown.

Scientists have suggested that the ground squirrel uses its tail to divert the rattlesnake's attention, encouraging the snake to strike at the less vulnerable tail rather than its body. Whatever the reason, the arms race between these two creatures is throwing up unexpected challenges for those who study animal behaviour.

A computer-controlled "robo-squirrel" is used to provoke a response from a rattlesnake in a laboratory-based arena at the University of California in Davis, USA. ▶

Species in extremes

Could the principles of evolution that gave rise to life on Earth be applied to life elsewhere in the universe? Life on our planet exists because of interplay between genetic scenarios, physiological and anatomical methods, and environmental challenges. Conditions on our planet have been changing continuously from the very beginning.

In the earliest days of life on our planet, a group of blue-green algae (known as cyanobacteria) adopted **photosynthesis** as a way of life. They absorbed light from the Sun in order to make their food, and spewed out oxygen into the atmosphere. This had catastrophic effects for life forms that had adapted to relying on other gases in the atmosphere, such as methane.

As a result, multicellular life spread across the surface of the planet. This caused other global changes that presented all of life with new environmental challenges. It means that the co-evolution of organisms and their environment has been a basic feature of all living systems.

Alien depths

Life survives and thrives in the most extraordinary places: in 110°C (230°F) hot springs, and the coldest regions of the Antarctic; under enormous pressure in the deepest parts of the ocean, and in the driest deserts; even in acid bogs, and areas exposed to high levels of radiation (such as at the site of the Chernobyl nuclear disaster in Ukraine, eastern Europe).

A brittlestar and limpets living on the shell of a vent mussel, which, in turn, lives beside a deep-sea hydrothermal vent or underwater hot spring.

A diver from an icebreaker research ship investigates life beneath summer ice floes in the Canada Basin sector of the Arctic Ocean.

All organisms are made up of almost identical **molecules**. Yet evolution has enabled life to survive even in these extreme environments.

About 2.5 km (1.6 miles) down in the deep, dark sea there is an entire living **ecosystem**. It doesn't rely on energy from the Sun, but from heat generated at the centre of the Earth. It thrives in conditions that would at first seem alien to life. Deep-sea, hydrothermal vents (underwater, hot springs) are colonised by: red tube worms, up to 2.4 m (8 ft.) long; giant clams and mussels, 25 cm (10 in.) across; white crabs; and snowball-like masses of Pompeii worms that sit with their heads in 20°C (68°F) water and tails in 70°C (158°F) water. The entire ecosystem is dependent on bacteria that make use of hydrogen sulphide in the scalding water. Conditions here are not dissimilar to those on the early Earth, when life started out on its four billion year evolutionary journey.

It is revelations like these that prompted NASA (National Aeronautics and Space Administration) scientists to create an "Astrobiology Roadmap". In the coming years, NASA-sponsored programmes at many universities and institutions are to explore three areas of research:

- "How does life begin and evolve?"
- "Does life exist elsewhere in the universe?"
- "What is the future of life on Earth and beyond?"

They are three of the most fundamental questions in nature. The answers could mean that our current view of biodiversity – the huge range of living things – has to encompass whole new communities of life forms that are beyond our most vivid imaginings.

TIMELINE

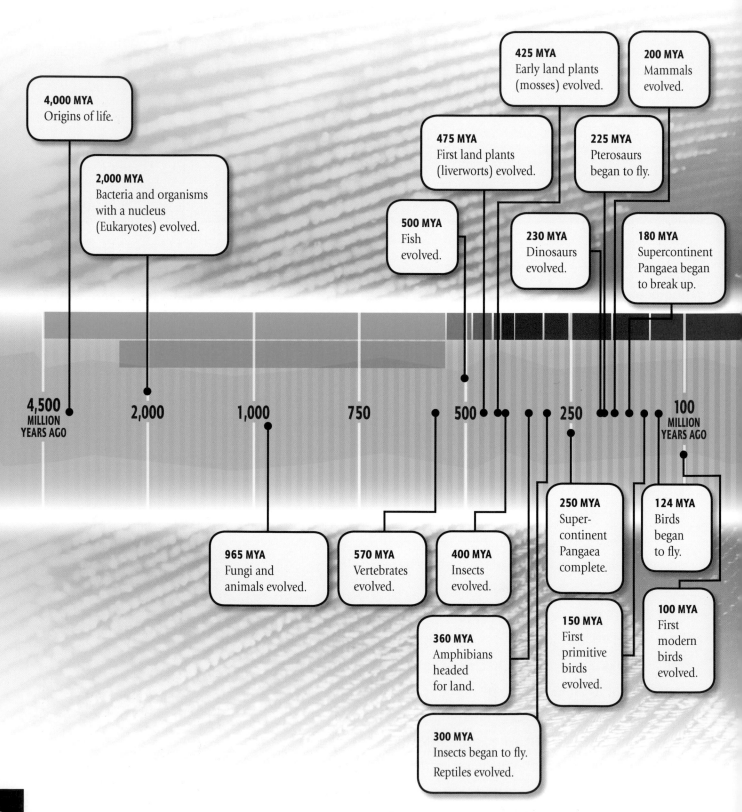

4,000 MYA
Origins of life.

2,000 MYA
Bacteria and organisms with a nucleus (Eukaryotes) evolved.

425 MYA
Early land plants (mosses) evolved.

200 MYA
Mammals evolved.

475 MYA
First land plants (liverworts) evolved.

225 MYA
Pterosaurs began to fly.

500 MYA
Fish evolved.

230 MYA
Dinosaurs evolved.

180 MYA
Supercontinent Pangaea began to break up.

4,500 MILLION YEARS AGO

2,000

1,000

750

500

250

100 MILLION YEARS AGO

965 MYA
Fungi and animals evolved.

570 MYA
Vertebrates evolved.

400 MYA
Insects evolved.

250 MYA
Super-continent Pangaea complete.

124 MYA
Birds began to fly.

360 MYA
Amphibians headed for land.

150 MYA
First primitive birds evolved.

100 MYA
First modern birds evolved.

300 MYA
Insects began to fly. Reptiles evolved.

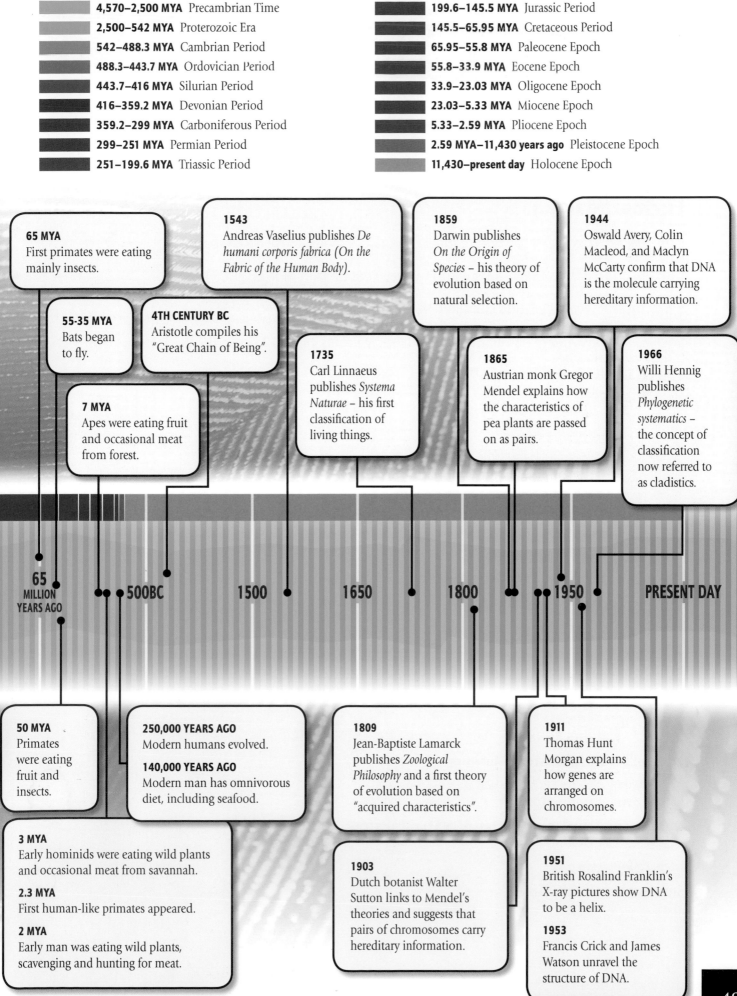

4,570–2,500 MYA Precambrian Time
2,500–542 MYA Proterozoic Era
542–488.3 MYA Cambrian Period
488.3–443.7 MYA Ordovician Period
443.7–416 MYA Silurian Period
416–359.2 MYA Devonian Period
359.2–299 MYA Carboniferous Period
299–251 MYA Permian Period
251–199.6 MYA Triassic Period

199.6–145.5 MYA Jurassic Period
145.5–65.95 MYA Cretaceous Period
65.95–55.8 MYA Paleocene Epoch
55.8–33.9 MYA Eocene Epoch
33.9–23.03 MYA Oligocene Epoch
23.03–5.33 MYA Miocene Epoch
5.33–2.59 MYA Pliocene Epoch
2.59 MYA–11,430 years ago Pleistocene Epoch
11,430–present day Holocene Epoch

65 MYA
First primates were eating mainly insects.

55-35 MYA
Bats began to fly.

4TH CENTURY BC
Aristotle compiles his "Great Chain of Being".

7 MYA
Apes were eating fruit and occasional meat from forest.

1543
Andreas Vaselius publishes *De humani corporis fabrica (On the Fabric of the Human Body)*.

1735
Carl Linnaeus publishes *Systema Naturae* – his first classification of living things.

1859
Darwin publishes *On the Origin of Species* – his theory of evolution based on natural selection.

1865
Austrian monk Gregor Mendel explains how the characteristics of pea plants are passed on as pairs.

1944
Oswald Avery, Colin Macleod, and Maclyn McCarty confirm that DNA is the molecule carrying hereditary information.

1966
Willi Hennig publishes *Phylogenetic systematics* – the concept of classification now referred to as cladistics.

65
MILLION YEARS AGO

500BC

1500

1650

1800

1950

PRESENT DAY

50 MYA
Primates were eating fruit and insects.

3 MYA
Early hominids were eating wild plants and occasional meat from savannah.

2.3 MYA
First human-like primates appeared.

2 MYA
Early man was eating wild plants, scavenging and hunting for meat.

250,000 YEARS AGO
Modern humans evolved.

140,000 YEARS AGO
Modern man has omnivorous diet, including seafood.

1809
Jean-Baptiste Lamarck publishes *Zoological Philosophy* and a first theory of evolution based on "acquired characteristics".

1903
Dutch botanist Walter Sutton links to Mendel's theories and suggests that pairs of chromosomes carry hereditary information.

1911
Thomas Hunt Morgan explains how genes are arranged on chromosomes.

1951
British Rosalind Franklin's X-ray pictures show DNA to be a helix.

1953
Francis Crick and James Watson unravel the structure of DNA.

FIND OUT MORE

Further reading:

Can You Tell a Skink from a Salamander?, Anna Claybourne (Raintree, 2005)

Classification of Life, Melissa Stewart (Twenty-First Century Books, 2007)

Eyewitness: Evolution, Linda Gamlin (DK Childrens, 2000)

So Simple a Beginning, edited and introduced by Professor E. O. Wilson (W. W. Norton, 2005)

The Evolution Book, Sara Stein (Workman, 1986)

To view:

Planet Earth, the complete BBC series (BBC Warner, 2007)

Websites:

Websites covering general evolution and biodiversity:

http://www.ucmp.berkeley.edu/index.php
University of California Museum of Palaeontology

http://evolution.berkeley.edu/evolibrary/home.php
University of California at Berkeley

http://www.nhm.ac.uk/
London's Natural History Museum

http://www.amnh.org/
New York's American Museum of Natural History

http://www.si.edu/
Smithsonian Institution

http://www.fieldmuseum.org/

Chicago's The Field Museum

http://www.darwinproject.ac.uk/

The Darwin Correspondence Project

http://darwin-online.org.uk/

The complete works of Charles Darwin online

http://www.literature.org/authors/darwin-charles/

Darwin's books

Websites covering life in space:

http://nai.nasa.gov/index.cfm

NASA Astrobiology Institute

Websites with biological science news:

http://news.bbc.co.uk/2/hi/science/nature/

http://www.sciencedaily.com/

http://sciencenow.sciencemag.org/

http://www.newscientist.com/news.ns

To research:

Why has the peppered moth controversy caused a flap?

The peppered moth story is not as straightforward as it seems at first. See if you can pick out fact from fiction. Check out the people involved: J. B. S. Haldane, J. W. Tutt, Bernard Kettlewell, Nico Tinbergen, J. W. Heslop-Harrison, Bruce Grant, L. M. Cook, Michael Majerus, Jerry Coyne, and Judith Hooper. What role did each of them play? What was the Industrial Revolution and what impact did it have on living things and the natural environment?

Bow down to the Red Queen Principle

You can find the Red Queen's statement relating to evolutionary competition in: *Through the Looking-Glass*, Lewis Carroll (first published by Macmillan, 1866)

Delve into the Galapagos

Explore the Galapagos Islands and discover which animals led Charles Darwin to his theory of evolution. Focus on the birds and tortoises. You can also check this website run by the Charles Darwin Foundation with a research station at the Galapagos Islands:

http://www.darwinfoundation.org/

Unravel unusual names

Evolutionary biology is scattered with strange characters. See what you can find out about the Red Queen, the Vicar of Bray, and Green-beard. What is their link with biology?

Are island animals a big (or small) deal?

Find out more about gigantism and dwarfism on islands, especially on Komodo, Indonesia. Why are Komodo dragons, the world's largest living monitor lizard, so large? With dwarf elephants extinct, on what do the dragons feed today? Where else in the world were there dwarf elephants?

GLOSSARY

adaptation a characteristic of an organism that enables it to be better suited to its environment

anatomy study of the parts and systems of living bodies

ancestor one from whom a person or other living thing is directly descended

arms race competition between two or more organisms or populations, such as a predator and prey, to get the upper hand

bacteria microorganisms that can exist either as independent organisms or as parasites

behaviour the actions or reactions of an organism in relation to the environment or other organisms

cell the smallest structural and functioning unit of a living thing that can be said to be alive

chromosome a single continuous piece of DNA (the blueprint of life) found in living cells, on which are found the genes

cladogram a tree-like diagram showing evolutionary relationships between living things

class a term in the classification of living things that is a level below "phylum" and above "order"

classification the method by which scientists group and categorise different living things

competition occurs when two or more organisms share a common demand for environmental resources that are in short supply, examples being food, shelter, nesting sites, and mates

disciplines bodies of knowledge given to or received by a learned person, such as a scientist

diversity of species variation of life forms in an ecosystem, biome or on the entire Earth, often referred to as "biodiversity"

DNA stands for deoxyribonucleic acid, which contains all the genetic instructions for the development and functioning of a living thing

ecologist a scientist who studies the interaction of living things and their environment

ecosystem a natural unit of all the living things in an area that interact not only together but also with the non-living parts of the environment

enzymes biological molecules that speed up or slow down the rate of chemical reactions

epoch a unit of the geological timescale; less than a "period"

extinction the ending of the existence of a species or group of living things, thus reducing biodiversity

family a term in the classification of living things that is below "order" and above "genus"

fossils the preserved remains or traces of once living things

gene a region on a chromosome corresponding to a unit of inheritance

generation a stage in the succession of natural descent. When advantageous characteristics are passed from one generation to the next it is known as "evolution".

genetics the study of heredity, variation in living things, and the mechanisms of inheritance

genus (pl. genera) a term in the classification of living things that is below "family" and above "species"

habitat the place where a particular organism lives

helix a three-dimensional twisted shape, like a twisted ladder

heredity the transfer of characteristics from one generation to the next, i.e. from parent to offspring, through their genes

hierarchy a system of organising living things by virtue of rank or status

inherited characteristics received from a parent or ancestor by genetic transmission

kingdom a term in the classification of living things that is below "domain" and above "phylum"

macroevolution refers to large-scale and long-term evolutionary changes that take place above species level

mammals vertebrate animals with sweat glands and hair, the females of which produce milk and suckle young

marsupial mammals in which the females have a pouch in which they rear their young during early infancy

microevolution refers to small-scale and short-term evolutionary changes that take place within a species or population

molecular biology the study of biology at the level of molecules

molecule a group of more than two atoms held together by strong chemical bonds

mutations changes to the sequences of genes of an organism

natural selection the process by which favourable inherited characteristics become more common and less favourable ones become less common in successive generations

nocturnal active mainly at night

order a term in classification of living things that is below "class" and above "family"

organism an individual living system, such as a plant, animal, bacterium, or fungi, that reacts to stimuli, reproduces, grows and maintains itself

palaeontology the study of prehistoric life forms through plant and animal fossils

penicillin a group of antibiotics used in the treatment of bacterial infections

photosynthesis the conversion of light energy from sunlight into chemical energy using carbon dioxide and water

phylum (pl. phyla) a term in the classification of living things that is below "kingdom" and above "class"

physiological relating to the mechanical, biochemical and physical functions of living organisms

population a collection of individuals of a particular species

predation a biological interaction in which an organism consumes another organism

predator an organism that consumes other organisms

prey an organism that is consumed by another organism

prowess possessing extraordinary ability

recessive a condition that occurs when an offspring receives two copies of a mutant gene, one copy from each parent

species one of the basic units of biological classification that includes organisms that are capable of breeding and producing viable offspring. In ranking it is below "genus".

specimen an individual or part of an individual that represents a group, such as a class, family, genus or species.

structural relating to systems that support and resist loads

survival of the fittest related to competition for survival or dominance which Darwin adopted as a synonym for "natural selection"

taxonomy the science of ordering and classification

INDEX